STAR SPANGLED

FAVORITES

Eleanor Burns   Sue Bouchard

Grant, Orion and Dylan
Stars in our lives

First printing November, 2002

Published by Quilt in a Day®, Inc.
1955 Diamond St, San Marcos, CA 92069

©2002 by Eleanor A. Burns Family Trust

ISBN 1-891776-12-6

Art Director Merritt Voigtlander

Contents

Introduction

My friend Sue and I have shared plenty of stories over coffee and apple pie. As mothers, quilters, and proud Americans, we have a lot to talk about!

We agree that we have been fortunate to raise our sons in the peace and freedom of this great country. I'm so proud of both my sons, Grant and Orion. Grant, the oldest, is now a successful business owner, while Orion has joined me in running Quilt in Day. Sue's son Dylan and my sons are great friends. I've enjoyed watching him grow up to be a fine young man.

After the events of September 11, I felt a special need to remember my American heritage. Now, more than ever, our freedom is something to be appreciated and celebrated. Sue and I worked together to bring you the eight patriotic projects in this new book. It's our quilters' way of honoring all that's good about our wonderful country.

Enjoy stitching up the dreams of our nation!

Eleanor Burns

Sue Bouchard

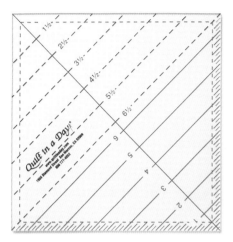

Seven of the projects in this book use spirited stars made from Flying Geese patches. Select from the projects on pages 20 – 69. Then turn to instructions in the front of the book to see how Sue and I make perfect points for our stars by using the 3" x 6" geese ruler from Quilt in a Day.

Another time saving ruler used for these projects is the 6½" Triangle Square Up, perfect for creating sharp points on the eagles' wings.

These are two rulers that belong in every quilter's collection of notions!

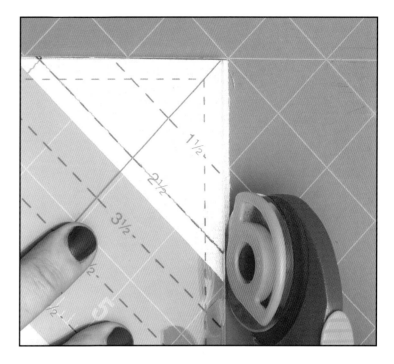

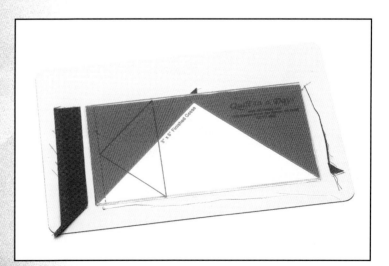

Making Dark Star Points or Light Geese

1. Place smaller light Background square right sides together and centered on larger dark square.

2" x 3½" Patch	3½" x 6½" Patch
4½" Background	7½" Background
6" Dark	9" Dark

2. Place 6" x 24" ruler on squares so ruler touches all four corners. Draw diagonal line across squares. Pin.

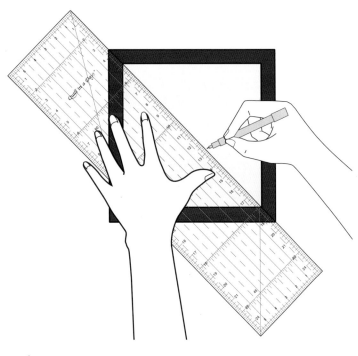

3. Sew **exactly** ¼" from both sides of drawn line. Use 15 stitches per inch or 2.0 on computerized machine. Assembly-line sew several squares. Press to set seam.

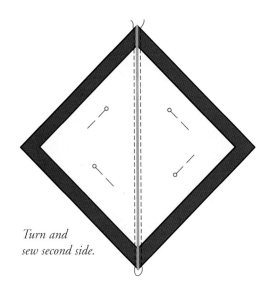

Turn and sew second side.

4. Remove pins. Cut on drawn line.

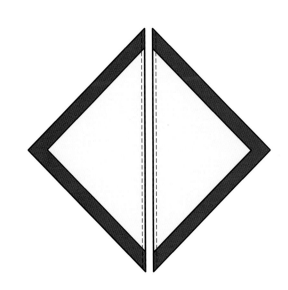

5. Place on pressing mat with **large triangle** on top. Press to set seam.

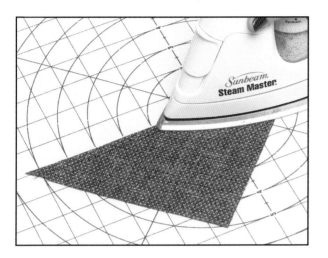

6. Open and press flat. Check that there are no tucks, and **seam is pressed toward larger triangle.**

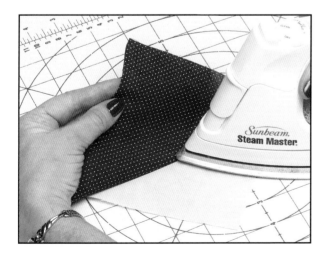

7. Place pieces right sides together so that opposite fabrics touch with dark matched to Background. Seams are parallel with each other.
Scrappy Points: See page 9.

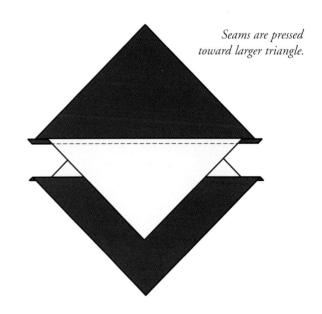

Seams are pressed toward larger triangle.

8. Match up outside edges. Notice that there is a gap between seams. **The seams do not match.**

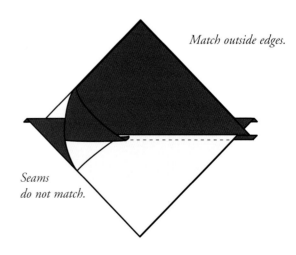

Match outside edges.

Seams do not match.

9. Draw a diagonal line across seams. Pin. Sew ¼" from both sides of drawn line. Hold seams flat with stiletto so seams do not flip. Press to set seam.

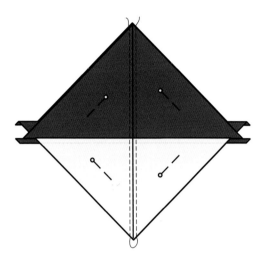

10. Cut on the drawn line.

11. Fold in half and clip to the stitching. This allows the seam allowance to be pressed away from Background.

12. From right side, press into one Background. Turn and press into second Background seam.

13. Turn over, and press on wrong side. At clipped seam, fabric is pressed away from Background.

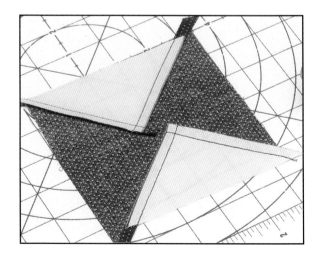

Making Scrappy Star Points

Instructions are the same as on pages 6 – 8 with the exception of placing two different fabrics right sides together.

For two color points opposite each other, make only one set.

For points with alternating colors, make two sets with same red and same blue.

Place remaining half of red with different blue.

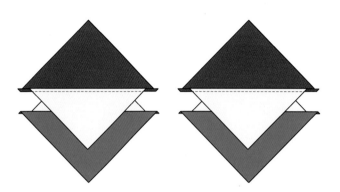

You end up with two different sets of points.

Two each

Two each

You end up with two sets of four points each for two stars.

Four each

Four each

Points are mirror image of each other.

Points are opposite each other.

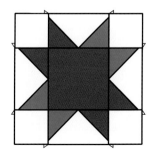

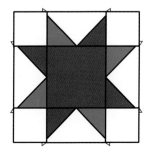

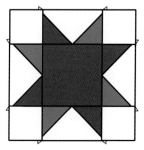

2" x 3½" Patches Finished at 1½" x 3"

Squaring Up with Small Geese Ruler

1. Line up ruler's **red lines** on 45° sewn lines. Line up dotted line with peak of triangle for ¼" seam allowance. Cut block in half to separate two patches.

Place red lines on seam.

2. Trim off excess fabric on right. Hold ruler securely on fabric so it will not shift while cutting.

Trim on right.

3. Turn patch around. **Do not turn ruler.** Trim off excess fabric on right and top.

4. Repeat with second half.

Trim to 2" x 3½".

Squaring Up without Geese Ruler

1. With a 6" x 12" ruler, line up the 45° line on a diagonal seam, and the ¼" line on the peak. Cut across, keeping an exact ¼" seam allowance beyond peak. Turn second piece and repeat.

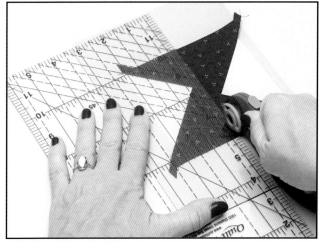

Cut block in half.

2. With the 6" square ruler, place the diagonal line on the seam. Line up the bottom edge of the patch with the 2" line on the ruler. Left edge should be slightly wider than 3½". Trim right and top edges.

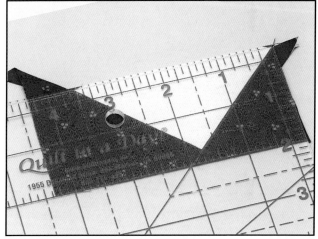

Trim off excess fabric on right.

3. Turn patch. **Do not turn ruler**. Line up left edge on 3½" line. Trim on right edge.

4. Repeat with second half.

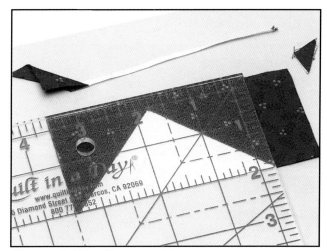

Turn patch. Trim off excess on right.

3½" x 6½" Patches Finished at 3" x 6"

Squaring Up with Geese Ruler

1. Line up ruler's **green lines** on 45° sewn lines. Line up dotted line with peak of triangle for the ¼" seam allowance.

2. Trim excess fabric on all four sides. Turn mat around while trimming.

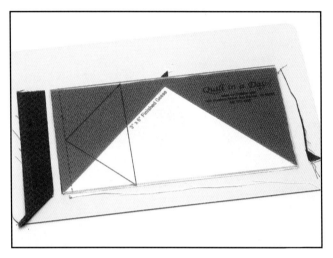

Squaring Up without Geese Ruler

1. With 6" x 12" ruler, line up 45° line on diagonal seam, and ¼" line on peak. Cut across, keeping an exact ¼" seam allowance beyond peak. Turn second piece and repeat.

2. With 12½" square ruler, place the diagonal line on seam. Line up bottom edge of patch with 3½" line on ruler. The left edge should be slightly wider than 6½". Trim right and top edge.

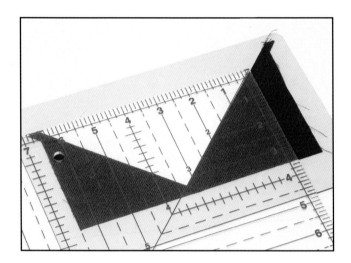

3. Turn patch. Do not turn ruler. Trim right edge to a perfect 3½" x 6½".

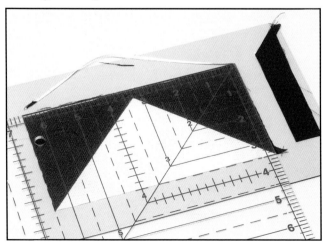

Making Stars

1. Lay out the Center square, Corner squares and Points.

6" Finished Star
2" x 3½" Points
3½" Center Square
2" Corner Squares

12" Finished Star
3½" x 6½" Points
6½" Center Square
3½" Corner Squares

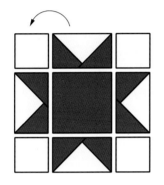

2. Flip middle row to left. Assembly-line sew all vertical seams.

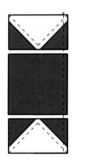 

3. Open and add right row.

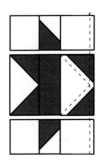

4. Sew first horizontal row, pressing seams toward Star Center, and away from the Star Points.

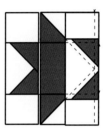

5. Sew second horizontal row, repeating seams. Set seams, open, and press.

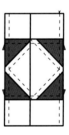

6. Check from wrong side. Horizontal seams should be pressed away from center. Press. Measure your block.

2" x 3½"   3½" x 6½"
6½" Square   12½" Square

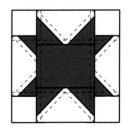

Making 12" Finished Double Star

1. Lay out 6½" Star with 3½" Corners and 3½" x 6½" Star Points. Turn 6½" Star with last seams in horizontal position.

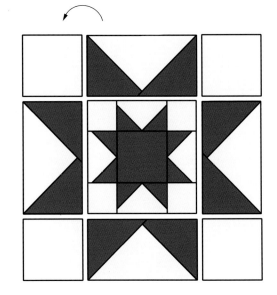

2. Flip middle row to left. Check horizontal seams on Star. Assembly-line sew all vertical seams.

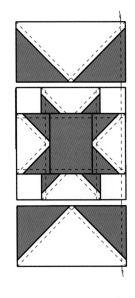

3. Open and add right row.

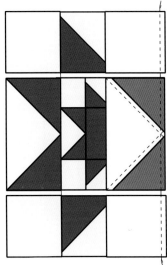

4. Sew first horizontal row, pressing seams toward Star, and away from Star points.

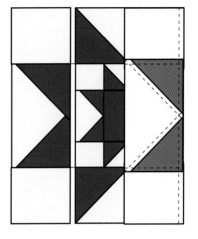

5. Sew second horizontal row, repeating seams. Set seams, open, and press.

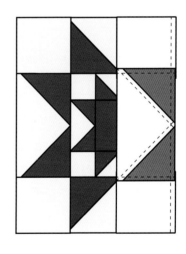

6. Check from wrong side. Horizontal seams should be pressed away from center.

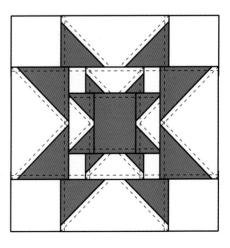

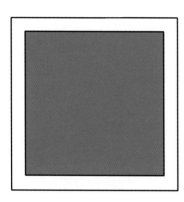

Making Light Star Points or Dark Geese

1. Place smaller dark square right sides together and centered on larger Background square.

   2" x 3½" Patch
   4½" Dark
   6" Background

   3½" x 6½" Patch
   7½" Dark
   9" Background

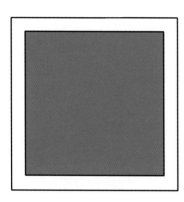

2. Place 6" x 24" ruler on squares so ruler touches all four corners. Draw diagonal line across squares. Pin.

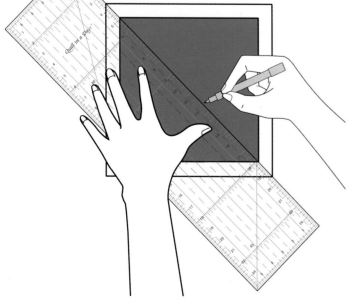

3. Sew **exactly** ¼" from drawn line. Use 15 stitches per inch or 2.0 on computerized machine. Assembly-line sew several squares. Press to set seam.

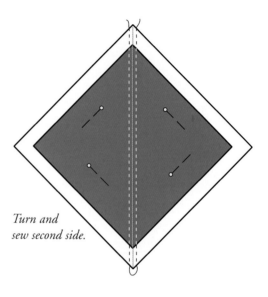

Turn and sew second side.

4. Remove pins. Cut on drawn line.

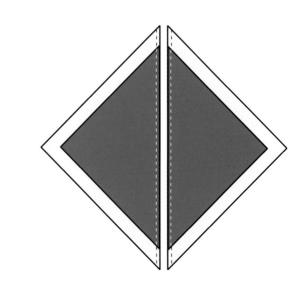

5. Place on pressing mat with **large triangle** on top. Press to set seam.

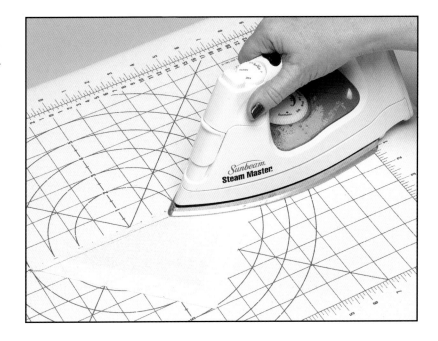

6. Open and press flat. Check that there are no tucks, and **seam is pressed toward larger triangle.**

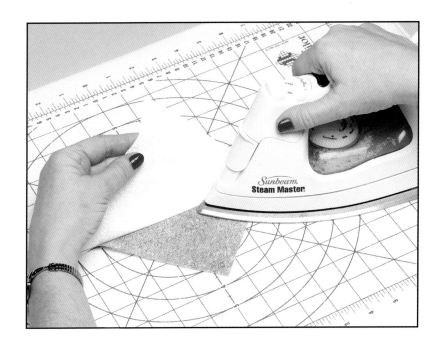

7. Place pieces right sides together so that opposite fabrics touch with dark matched to Background. **Seams are parallel with each other.**

Seams are pressed toward larger triangle.

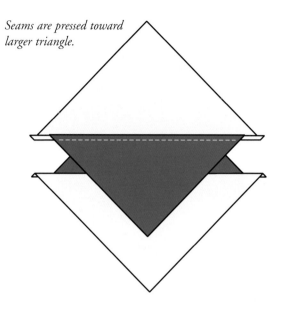

8. Match up outside edges. Notice that there is a gap between seams. **The seams do not lock.**

Match outside edges.

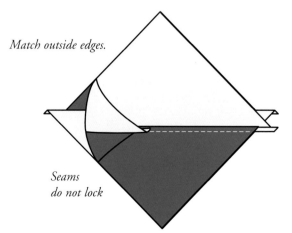

Seams do not lock

9. Draw a diagonal line across seams. Pin. Sew ¼" from both sides of drawn line. Hold seams flat with stiletto so seams do not flip. Press to set seam.

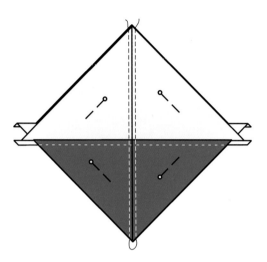

10. Cut on the drawn line.

11. Fold in half and clip to the stitching. This allows the seam allowance to be pressed away from the dark.

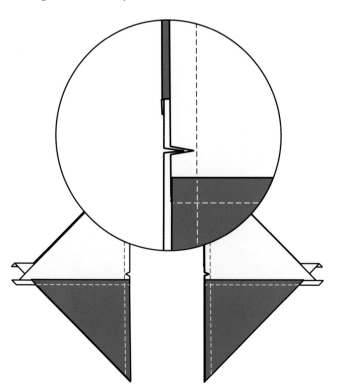

12. From right side, press into one dark. Turn and press into second dark seam.

13. Turn over, and press on wrong side. At clipped seam, fabric is pressed away from the dark. Square up following directions on pages 10 – 12.

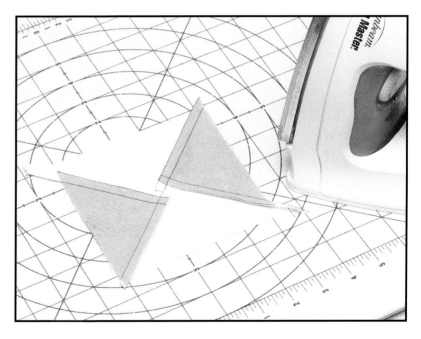

Patriotic Eagle

Sue Bouchard
Approximate Finished Size 30" x 34"

The Eagle feather tells the story of life. It represents duality, as light and dark, male and female, summer and winter, peace and war, life and death. Native American traditionalists look upon the eagle feather as a sacred symbol of the balance necessary for the Circle of Life to continue. Duality is important in fabrics selected for our quilts as well.

Patriotic Eagle

Dark Red   ¼ yd
Top of Wings
(1) 6" square
Beak
(1) 2" square
Head
(1) 1½" x 2½"
(1) 1½" x 6½"

Medium Red   ¼ yd
Feather Tips
(1) 6" square

Background   ⅝ yd
Eagle
(1) 6½" strip cut into
   (4) 6½" squares
   (2) 6" squares
(1) 2½" strip cut into
   (6) 2½" squares
   (4) 2½" x 6½"
Stripe Border
(3) 2½" strips

First Blue Print   ½ yd
Body
(1) 2½" strip cut into
   (2) 2½" squares
   (2) 2½" x 4½"
Tail
(2) 2½" x 5½"
(1) 1½" x 6½"
Stripe Border
(2) 2½" strips
(1) 4½" strip cut into
   (4) 4½" x 6½"
Body
(2) 3½" squares

Second Blue Solid or Tone on Tone ⅛ yd
Body
(1) 3½" x 6½"
Tail
(2) 1½" x 6"

Third Blue   ½ yd
Lattice
(4) 2½" strips
Stars
(3) 4½" squares
(1) 2" strip cut into
   (12) 2" squares

Yellow   ¼ yd
Star Points
(3) 6" squares
Star Centers
(3) 3½" squares

Finishing
Non-woven Fusible Interfacing ¼ yd
(1) 7" square

Binding ⅜ yd
(4) 2¾" strips

Backing 1 yd

Batting 38" x 42"

Making Pieced Triangle Squares for Wings

1. Place one Background 6" square right
   sides together to Feather Tip 6" square.
   Repeat with Top of Wing 6" square.
   Draw "X" on wrong side of Background
   squares.

Dark Red
Top of Wings and Head
One is extra.

Medium Red
Feather Tips

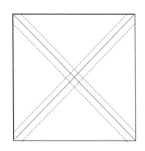

2. Sew ¼" from both diagonal lines. Set
   seams and cut horizontally and vertically
   at 3". Cut on both diagonal lines.

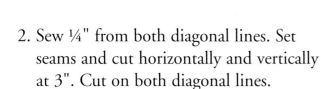

3. Place 2½" line on 6½" Triangle Square
   Up Ruler **on stitches**. Trim excess to
   2½" square.

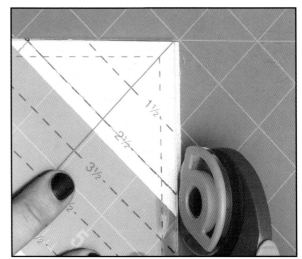

2½" line on top of stitches.

4. Trim off tips.

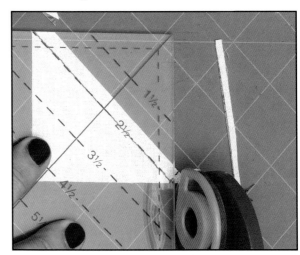

5. Set seams with darkest on top. Open,
   and press seams toward dark.

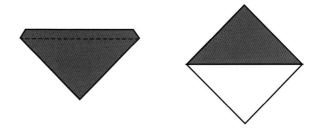

Making the Upper Left Wing

1. Lay out pieces for Left Upper Wing section.

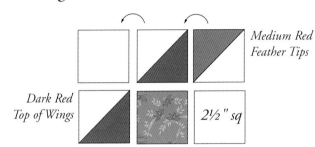

Medium Red Feather Tips

2½" sq

Dark Red Top of Wings

2. Sew pieces together. Press seams toward 2½" Corner Squares.

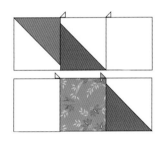

3. Sew rows together.

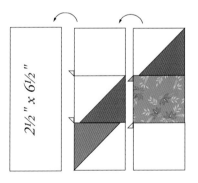

2½" x 6½"

4. Press seams away from middle row.

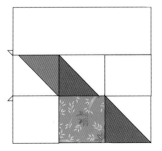

Making the Upper Right Wing

1. Lay out pieces for Right Upper Wing section.

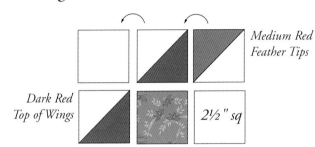

Medium Red Feather Tips

Dark Red Top of Wings

2½" sq

2. Sew pieces together. Press seams toward 2½" Corner Squares.

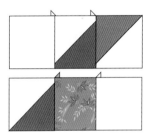

3. Sew rows together.

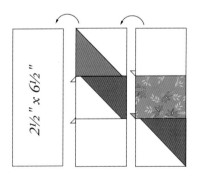

2½" x 6½"

4. Press seams away from middle row.

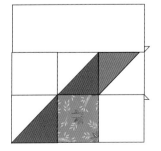

Completing the Center Body

1. On the wrong side of (2) 3½" Print squares, draw diagonal lines.

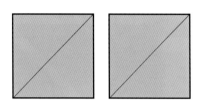

2. Place one marked square on 3½" x 6½" Body right sides together. Sew on drawn line.

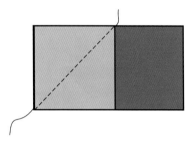

3. Trim to ¼". Press seam away from Body.

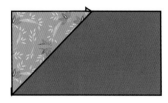

4. Repeat process with remaining 3½" Print square.

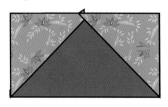

5. Repress one patch for locking seams. Sew Row 1 together. Press seams toward Head.

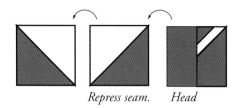

Repress seam.   Head

6. Lay out pieces for Center Body section, and sew rows together.

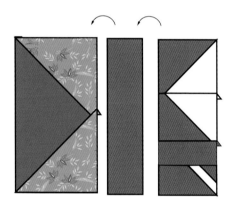

7. Press seams toward middle row.

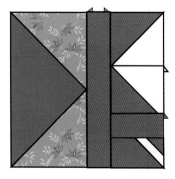

Making the Pieced Tail

1. Lay out Tail strips. Keeping the top edge even, sew pieces together.

2½" x 5½" 1½" x 6" 1½" x 6½" 1½" x 6" 2½" x 5½"

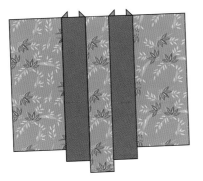

2. Set and press seams toward Solid Fabric.

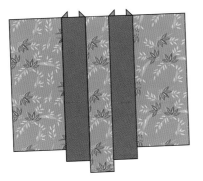

3. Trace Tail Pattern on smooth side of fusible interfacing. (Pattern on page 31.)

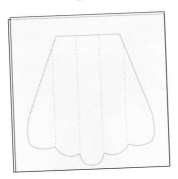

4. Place bumpy side of interfacing on Pieced Tail fabrics. Line up lines on interfacing with seam lines. Using 18-20 stitches per inch, **sew on outside lines of Tail.**

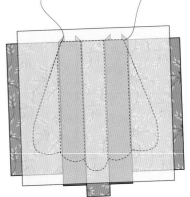

5. Trim to ⅛" and clip curves. Turn right side out.

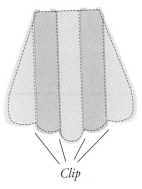

Clip

6. Center sides on 6½" Background square, and fuse in place.

7. Hand stitch around outside edge or machine blind hem stitch with invisible thread.

Bald Eagle

C...

1. I
t
t

2. I
s

3. Se
to
Pr
Ro

4. Sew
awa

Sue Bouchard　　　　　*Approximate Finished Size 30" x 34"*

Our founding fathers argued for years about what our national emblem should be. Benjamin Franklin thought the "national bird" should be the wild turkey. Others thought that an eagle stood for freedom, strength, and courage. It's also a native bird, found only in North America. Despite their reputation as chicken thieves around farms, in 1782, the bald eagle was chosen as a symbol of this nation.

A few eagles have become American heroes. Old Abe, the mascot of a Wisconsin regiment during the Civil War, traveled with the troops. He was a constant target of enemy riflemen, but survived 42 battle engagements. A turkey wouldn't have lasted as long!

First Black Solid or Tone on Tone   ¾ yd

Wings
- (2) 6" squares

Body
- (1) 2½" strip cut into
    - (2) 2½" squares
    - (1) 1½" x 6½"

Tail
- (2) 2½" x 3¾"
- (1) 1½" x 4¾"

Body
- (2) 3½" squares

Lattice
- (4) 2½" strips

Stars
- (1) 2" strip cut into
    - (12) 2" squares
- (3) 4½" squares

Second Black Print   ½ yd

Body
- (1) 3½" x 6½"
- (2) 2½" x 4½"

Tail
- (2) 1½" x 4¼"

Stripe Border
- (2) 2½" strips
- (1) 4½" strip cut into
    - (4) 4½" x 6½"

Yellow   ¼ yd

Star Points
- (3) 6" squares

Star Centers
- (3) 3½" squares

White   ⅛ yd

Back of Head
- (1) 3" square

Beak
- (1) 2" square

Head
- (1) 1½" x 2½"

Tail
- (2) 1½" x 2¼"
- (2) 2½" x 2¼"
- (1) 1½" x 2¼"

Sky Blue Background   ⅝ yd

Eagle
- (1) 6½" strip cut into
    - (4) 6½" squares
    - (2) 6" squares
- (1) 2½" strip cut into
    - (6) 2½" squares
    - (4) 2½" x 6½"

Stripe Border
- (3) 2½" strips

Back of Head
- (1) 3" square

Finishing

Non-woven Fusible Interfacing   ¼ yd
- (1) 7" square

Binding   ⅜ yd
- (4) 2¾" strips

Backing   1 yd

Batting   38" x 42"

Instructions for the Bald Eagle are the same as the Patriotic Eagle on pages 22 – 31 with these exceptions.

 **Making Pieced Triangle Squares**

1. **Wings:** Place two Sky Blue 6" squares with two First Black 6" squares. Draw "X" on wrong side of Sky squares.

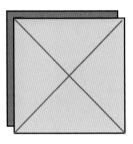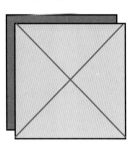

2. Sew ¼" from diagonal lines. Set seams and cut horizontally and vertically at 3". Cut on both diagonal lines.

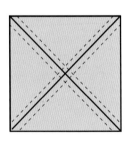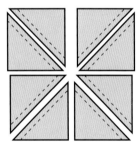

3. **Back of Head:** Place one 3" white square right sides together to one Sky Blue 3" square. Draw one diagonal line.

Head

4. Sew ¼" from diagonal line and cut.

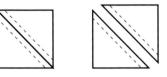

5. Place 2½" line on 6½" Triangle Square Up Ruler on stitches. Trim excess to 2½" square.

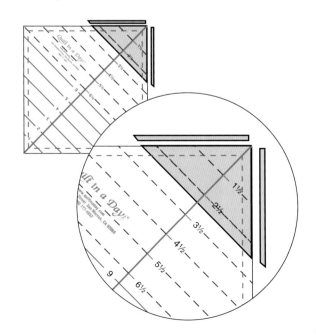

6. Trim off tips.

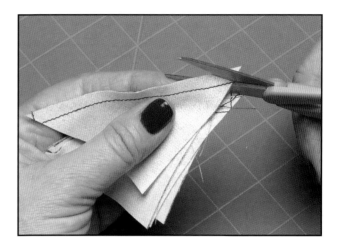

7. **Wings:** Set seams with darkest on top. Open, and press seams toward dark.

8. **Back of Head:** Press seam toward Sky.

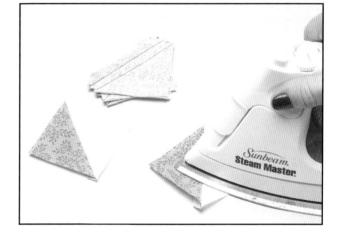

Making Upper and Middle Wings

1. Follow instructions for Upper Wings, page 23, substituting First Black Pieced Triangle Squares.

2. Follow instructions for Middle Wings, page 24, substituting First Black Pieced Triangle Squares.

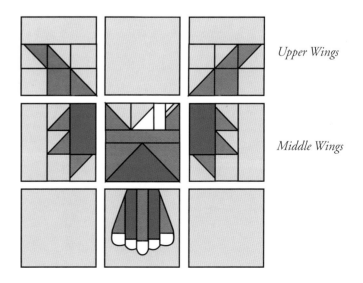

Upper Wings

Middle Wings

Making the Head

1. On the wrong side of the 2" Beak square, draw a diagonal line.

2. Place Beak over Sky half of Pieced Triangle Square right sides together.

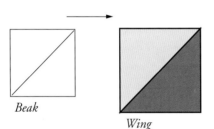

3. Sew on drawn line.

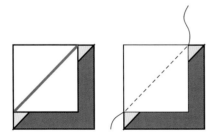

4. Cut off excess. Press seam toward Beak.

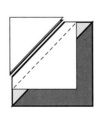

5. Turn 1½" x 2½" Head rectangle wrong side up.

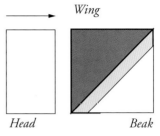

6. Place 1½" x 2½" Head rectangle over the largest triangle. Only a small portion of the Large Triangle is showing. Sew ¼" from edge.

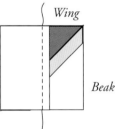

7. Trim excess.

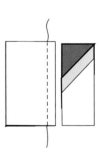

8. Press seam under rectangle.

9. Continue with Completing the Center Body, page 26.

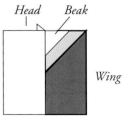

Making the Bald Eagle Pieced Tail

1. Lay out Tail strips. Sew on white strips, and press seams toward dark. Keeping the top edge even, sew pieces together.

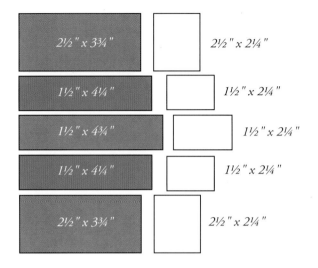

2. Set and press seams toward 1½" strips.

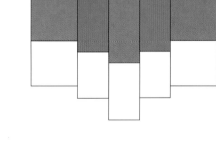

3. Trace the Tail Pattern on smooth side of fusible interfacing.

4. Continue on page 27.

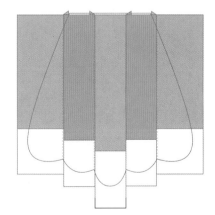

Stars & Bars Tablerunner

Welcome guests with coffee and apple pie, on a table warmed by a patriotic Stars & Bars tablerunner. Apple pie was a favorite dessert in England during the reign of Elizabeth I. The colonists brought apples with them to the New World and planted the first orchard in Massachusetts around 1625. The warm summers and cold winters of New England helped farmers develop sweeter varieties of the fruit. Apples became a staple in the colonial diet, in part because they could be dried and stored for up to six months.

Stars & Bars
Tablerunner

4 Blue Stars
44 Red Geese

Approximate
Finished Size
18" x 36"

Stars & Bars
Tablerunner

4 Scrappy Stars
22 Red Geese
22 Blue Geese

Approximate
Finished Size
18" x 36"

Stars & Bars
Tablerunner

6 Blue Stars
68 Red Geese

Approximate
Finished Size
18" x 54"

Red   1/3 yd

Flying Geese
(2) 4½" strips cut into
(11) 4½" squares

White   ¾ yd
Star Corners
(1) 2" strip cut into
(16) 2" squares
Star Points
(1) 4½" strip cut into
(4) 4½" squares
Background for Flying Geese
(2) 6" strips cut into
(11) 6" squares
Inside Border
(2) 2" strips

Blue   ¾ yd
Star Centers and Bars
(1) 3½" strip cut into
(4) 3½" squares
(3) 3½" x 6½" strips
Star Points
(1) 6" strip cut into
(4) 6" squares
Outside Borders
(3) 2" strips
Binding
(3) 3" strips

Finishing

Backing ⅝ yd
Batting 22" x 40"

Red   (6) 1/3 yd pieces

Star Points
(2) different 6" squares
Star Centers
(2) different 3½" squares
Flying Geese
(6) different 4½" squares
Bars
(3) 3½" x 6½" strips
Outside Borders
(3) 2" strips from one
Binding
(3) 3" strips from one

Off-White   ¾ yd
Star Corners
(1) 2" strip cut into
(16) 2" squares
Star Points
(1) 4½" strip cut into
(4) 4½" squares
Background for Flying Geese
(2) 6" strips cut into
(12) 6" squares
Inside Border
(2) 2" strips

Blue   (6) 1/3 yd pieces
Star Points
(2) different 6" squares
Star Centers
(2) different 3½" squares
Flying Geese
(6) different 4½" squares

Finishing

Backing ⅝ yd
Batting 22" x 40"

Red   ½ yd

Flying Geese
(3) 4½" strips cut into
(17) 4½" squares

White   1 yd
Star Corners
(2) 2" strips cut into
(24) 2" squares
Star Points
(1) 4½" strip cut into
(6) 4½" squares
Background for Flying Geese
(3) 6" strips cut into
(17) 6" squares
Inside Border
(3) 2" strips

Blue   1⅛ yds
Star Center and Bars
(2) 3½" strips cut into
(6) 3½" squares
(5) 3½" x 6½" strips
Star Points
(1) 6" strip cut into
(6) 6" squares
Outside Borders
(4) 2" strips
Binding
(4) 3" strips

Finishing

Backing ¾ yd
Batting 22" x 58"

Making Blue Stars

1. Place 4½" white squares right sides together and centered on 6" blue squares. Make one set for each Star.

2. Follow instructions for making 2" x 3½" Dark Star Points on pages 6 – 11.

3. Make 6" Stars following directions on page 13.

Four Stars
Four sets

Six Stars
Six sets

Making Red Geese

1. Place 4½" red squares right side together and centered on 6" white squares.

2. Follow instructions for making 2" x 3½" Dark Geese on pages 16 – 19.

Four Stars
Eleven sets

Six Stars
Seventeen sets

3. Divide Geese into two equal stacks.

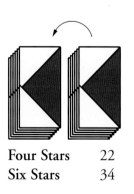

Four Stars   22
Six Stars   34

Making Scrappy Stars

1. Place 4½" off-white squares right sides together and centered on (2) 6" blue squares and (2) 6" red squares.

2. Follow instructions for making 2" x 3½" Dark Star Points on pages 6 – 11. See Scrappy Star Points on page 9.

3. Make 6" Stars following directions on page 13.

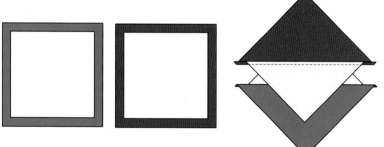

Making Scrappy Geese

1. Place (6) 4½" red squares and (6) 4½" blue squares right side together and centered on 6" off-white squares.

2. Follow instructions for making 2" x 3½" Dark Geese patches on pages 16 – 19.

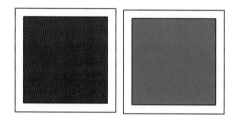

3. Divide Geese into two equal stacks.

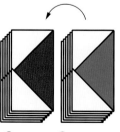

Scrappy Stars
Red 22
Blue 22

Sewing Geese Together

1. Assembly-line sew into pairs, and clip apart.

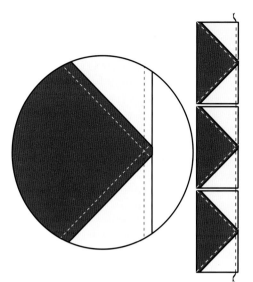

2. Continue to assembly-line sew into two sets.

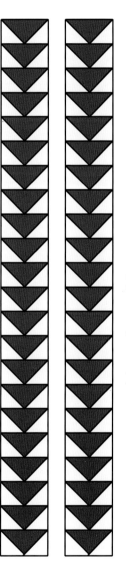

Example is for Four Star Tablerunner.

Four Blue Stars
Two sets of 22

Six Blue Stars
Two sets of 34

Four Scrappy Stars
Two sets of 22
Alternate between
red and blue

3. Press seams toward points of Geese.

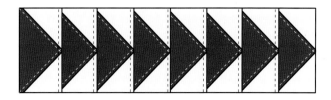

Finishing Tablerunner

1. Lay out Stars with 3½" x 6½" Bars. Assembly-line sew.

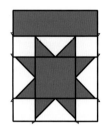

2. Set seams with Bars on top. Open, and press toward Bars.

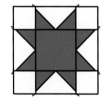

3. Sew sets together with remaining Star.

4. Press seams toward Bars.

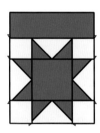

Example is for Four Star Tablerunner.

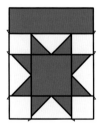

Scrappy Stars

Alternate between Stars with red centers and Stars with blue centers.

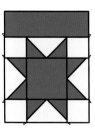

5. Cut white 2" Inside Border strips same length. Pin, and sew.

6. Set seams with Inside Border on top. Open, and press seams toward Border.

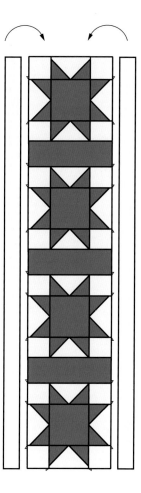

7. Pin and sew Geese to Inside Borders. Point one set of Geese up, and one set down.

8. Press seams toward Inside Border.

9. Measure, pin, and sew Outside Border.

10. Follow **Finishing Instructions** on pages 73 – 77.

12" Scrappy Stars

Teresa Varnes   *Approximate Finished Size 74" x 91"*

6" Scrappy Stars

Eleanor Burns   *Approximate Finished Size 41" x 49"*

Stars & Bars Quilts

At the battle of Antietam, on September 17, 1862, Clara Barton brought a wagonload of bandages and medical supplies that she had personally collected to aid the soldiers. She worked without stopping for the rest of the war, at times caring for the wounded of both sides. In later years, a monument was raised here in honor of this "Angel of the Battlefield." The Stars & Bars in your quilts help to commemorate the War Between the States.

6" Scrappy Stars

Red — Six ¼ yd Pieces

Star Centers
(1) 3½" square from each

Star Points
(1) 6" square from each

Flying Geese
(1) 4½" square from each
plus one more of favorite

Red Print — ⅓ yd

Bars
(3) 3½" strips cut into
(15) 3½" x 6½" strips

Off-White — 1⅜ yds

Star Corners
(3) 2" strips cut into
(48) 2" squares

Star Points
(2) 4½" strips cut into
(12) 4½" squares

Background for Flying Geese
(2) 6" strips cut into
(14) 6" squares

Inside Borders
(8) 2" strips

Blue — Six ¼ yd Pieces

Star Centers
(1) 3½" square from each

Star Points
(1) 6" square from each

Flying Geese
(1) 4½" square from each
plus one more of favorite

Blue Print — 1⅛ yds

Outside Border
(5) 4½" strips

Binding
(5) 3" strips

Finishing

Backing 1½ yds

Batting 45" x 54"

12" Scrappy Stars

Red — Six ⅓ yd Pieces

Star Centers
(1) 6½" square from each

Star Points
(1) 9" square from each

Flying Geese
(1) 7½" square from each
plus one more of favorite

Red Print — 1 yd

Bars
(5) 6½" strips cut into
(15) 6½" x 12½" strips

Off-White — 4 yds

Star Corners
(5) 3½" strips cut into
(48) 3½" squares

Star Points
(3) 7½" strips cut into
(12) 7½" squares

Background for Flying Geese
(4) 9" strips cut into
(14) 9" squares

Inside Borders
(16) 3½" strips

Blue — Six ⅓ yd Pieces

Star Centers
(1) 6½" square from each

Star Points
(1) 9" square from each

Flying Geese
(1) 7½" square from each
plus one more of favorite

Blue Print — 2⅛ yds

Outside Border
(8) 6" strips

Binding
(8) 3" strips

Finishing

Backing 6 yds

Batting 80" x 100"

Making Twelve Scrappy Stars

1. Place off-white squares right sides together and centered on red and blue squares.

   6" Stars

       (6) 4½" squares off-white and (6) 6" red

       (6) 4½" squares off-white and (6) 6" blue

   12" Stars

       (6) 7½" squares off-white and (6) 9" red

       (6) 7½" squares off-white and (6) 9" blue

Make six   *Make six*

2. Follow instructions for making Dark Star Points on pages 6 – 12. Place two pairs of same red and same blue patches right sides together, and continue as instructed.

   6" Stars

       2" x 3½" Star Points

   12" Stars

       3½" x 6½" Star Points

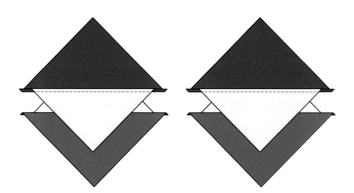

3. Square up Star Points with Geese ruler.

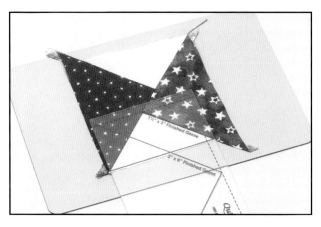

4. Follow instructions for sewing Stars together on page 13.

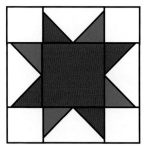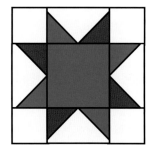

Six with red centers   *Six with blue centers*

Making 26 Red Geese and 26 Blue Geese

1. Place red and blue squares centered on off-white squares right sides together.

   Geese for 6" Stars
   > (7) 4½" squares red and (7) 6" off-white
   > (7) 4½" squares blue and (7) 6" off-white

   Geese for 12" Stars
   > (7) 7½" squares red and (7) 9" off-white
   > (7) 7½" squares blue and (7) 9" off-white

Make seven   *Make seven*

2. Follow instructions for making Dark Geese on pages 16 – 19.

   Geese for 6" Stars
   > 2" x 3½" Patch

   Geese for 12" Stars
   > 3½" x 6½" Patch

3. Divide Geese into a red stack and a blue stack. Place twenty-six in each stack. Two of each color are extra.

4. Assembly-line sew into pairs, and clip apart.

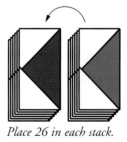

Place 26 in each stack.

5. Continue to assembly-line sew into two sets of twenty-six.

6. Press seams toward points of Geese.

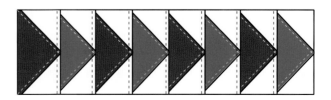

Thirteen Colony Quilts

Teresa Varnes

Eleanor Burns

Show your pride by making thirteen star quilts in patriotic scrappy, classic red and white, or traditional blue and white. The pattern itself, the Sawtooth Saw, is ancient. Inspiration for the name Sawtooth came from admiration for the hard working carpenter and his saw in colonial times.

Ruth Finley, author of *Old Patchwork Quilts* published in 1929, referred to this pattern as the Rising Star. Ladies Art Company from St Louis, Missouri, appropriately called it Stars and Squares.

Teresa Varnes   *Approximate Finished Size 38" x 38"*

Thirteen Colony Quilt

Light Background

White   1⅛ yds

Corners
(3) 2" strips cut into
(52) 2" squares

Star Background
(2) 4½" strips cut into
(13) 4½" squares

Solid Squares
(2) 6½" strips cut into
(12) 6½" squares
(cut later)

Borders
(4) 2" strips

Red   1½ yds

Center Square
(2) 3½" strips cut into
(13) 3½" squares

Star Points
(2) 6" strips cut into
(13) 6" squares

Borders
(8) 2" strips

Binding
(4) 3" strips

Finishing

Backing
1¼ yds
Batting
45" x 45"

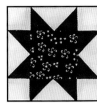

Thirteen Colony Quilt

Scrappy

White   1¼ yds

Corners
(3) 2" strips cut into
(52) 2" squares

Star Background
(2) 4½" strips cut into
(13) 4½" squares

Solid Squares
(2) 6½" strips cut into
(12) 6½" squares
(cut later)

Borders
(4) 2" strips

Red (6) fat eighths and ⅓ yd

Center Square
(1) 3½" square from each
(7) 3½" squares

Star Points
(1) 6" square from each
(6) 6" squares

Borders
(4) 2" strips

Blue (6) fat eighths and ⅔ yd

Center Square
(1) 3½" square from each
(6) 3½" squares

Star Points
(1) 6" square from each
(7) 6" squares

Borders
(4) 2" strips

Binding
(4) 3" strips

Finishing

Backing
1¼ yds
Batting
45" x 45"

Thirteen Colony Quilt

Dark Background

Off-White   1 yd

Center Square
(2) 3½" strip cut into
(13) 3½" squares

Star Points
(2) 6" strips cut into
(13) 6" squares

Borders
(4) 2" strips

Blue   1¾ yds

Corners
(3) 2" strips cut into
(52) 2" squares

Star Background
(2) 4½" strips cut into
(13) 4½" squares

Solid Squares
(2) 6½" strips cut into
(12) 6½" squares
(cut later)

Borders
(8) 2" strips

Binding
(4) 3" strips

Finishing

Backing   1¼ yds

Batting   45" x 45"

Mitering Corners

1. **Mark dots ¼" from all four corners on quilt top.**

2. Center Border strips on sides. Allow 6" at top and 6" at bottom for miter.

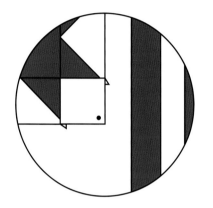

3. Flip Borders right sides together and pin, beginning at ¼" mark.

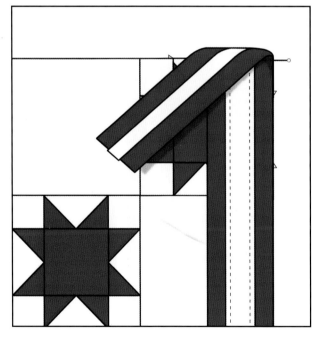

4. Sew Borders to sides, leaving ¼" open. Set seams with Borders on top. Open, and press toward Borders. Flip side Borders out of way.

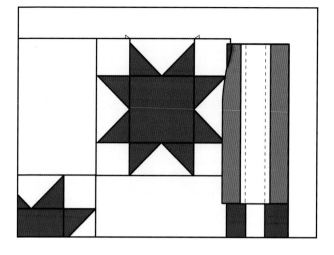

5. Center top and bottom Borders to quilt. Allow 6" to extend on both sides.

6. Flip Borders right sides together and pin, beginning at ¼" mark. Sew, leaving ¼" open on both ends.

7. Set seams with Borders on top, open, and press toward Borders.

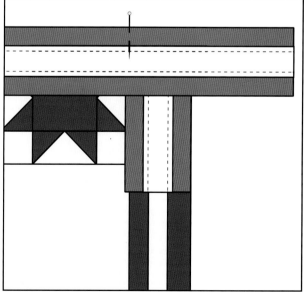

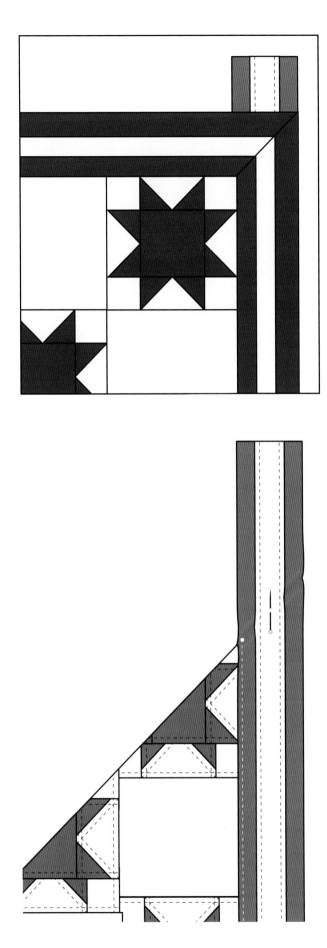

8. Place corner on pressing mat. Lay bottom strip out flat. Fold top strip under at 45° angle. Match seams on strips. Press. Check angle with 6½" Triangle Square Up ruler.

9. Carefully open pressed corner. Pin on creased line, matching seams. Sew on creased line beginning at open ¼". Open and check that seams line up.

10. Trim ¼" from seam.

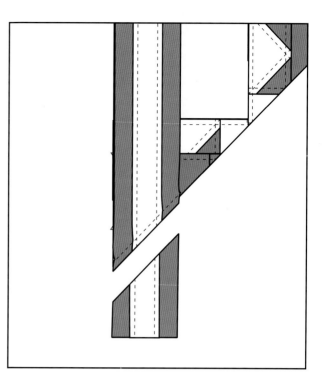

11. Press seam open. Trim tips from corner.

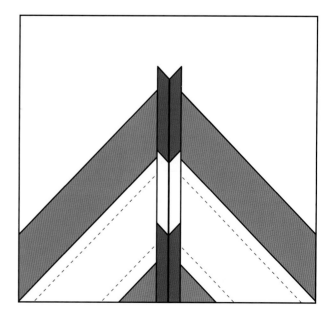

Heritage Star Quilts

Two Color

Teresa Varnes
Approximate Finished Size 68" x 83"

Many of the early symbols of our nation are public monuments today. One of the most memorable symbols of democracy, Mount Rushmore, was sculpted between 1927 and 1940. Four of our greatest presidents were chosen to represent the first 150 years of American history. Create your own symbol of American heritage with a patriotic quilt of stars within stars.

Scrappy

Sue Bouchard

58

Two Color

Large Star Points
(3) 9" strips cut into
(12) 9" squares

Small Star Points
(2) 6" strips cut into
(12) 6" squares

Strip Border and Nine Patches
(15) 2" strips

Binding
(8) 3" strips

White   5 yds

Large Stars
(3) 7½" strips cut into
(12) 7½" squares

Large Star Corners
(5) 3½" strips cut into
(48) 3½" squares

Small Stars
(2) 4½" strips cut into
(12) 4½" squares

Small Star Corners
(3) 2" strips cut into
(48) 2" squares

Small Star Center
(2) 3½" strips cut into
(12) 3½" squares

Lattice and Cornerstones
(14) 3½" strips cut into
(20) 3½" squares
(31) 3½" x size of Block – cut later

Strip Border and Nine Patches
(8) 2" strips

Outside Border
(7) 6" strips

Finishing

Backing 5 yds
Batting 76" x 90"

Scrappy

6 Reds and 6 Blues ⅓ yd or Fat Quarters

Cut from each
Large Star Points
(1) 9" square

Small Star Points
(1) 6" square

Small Star Center
(1) 3½" square

Background #1   1 yd

Small Stars
(2) 4½" strips cut into
(12) 4½" squares

Small Star Corners
(3) 2" strips cut into
(48) 2" squares

Strip Border and Nine Patches
(8) 2" strips

Background #2   4 yds

Large Stars
(3) 7½" strips cut into
(12) 7½" squares

Large Star Corners
(5) 3½" strips cut into
(48) 3½" squares

Lattice and Cornerstones
(14) 3½" strips cut into
(20) 3½" squares
(31) 3½" x size of Block – cut later

Outside Border
(7) 6" strips

Blue   1 yd

Strip Border and Nine Patches
(15) 2" strips

Finishing

Binding ¾ yd
(8) 3" strips
Backing 5 yds
Batting 76" x 90"

Making Twelve Small Stars

1. Place twelve light 4½" squares right sides together and centered on twelve dark 6" squares.

Two Color

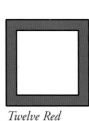

Twelve Red and White

Scrappy

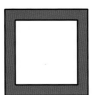

Background #1 and Six Red

Background #1 and Six Blue

2. Make 2" x 3½" Dark Star Points following directions on pages 6 – 12.

3. Sew 6" Stars together following directions on page 13.

Two Color

Twelve Red and White

Scrappy

Six Red
Six Blue

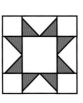

Making Large Star Points

1. Place twelve light 7½" squares right sides together and centered on twelve dark 9" squares.

Two Color

Twelve Red and White

Scrappy

Background #2 and Six Red

Background #2 and Six Blue

2. Make 3½" x 6½" Dark Star Points following directions on pages 6 – 12.

3. Make 12" Finished Double Star following directions on pages 14 – 15.

Two Color

Twelve Red and White 6" Stars
Red 3½" x 6½" Points
3½" Corner Squares

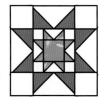

Scrappy

Six Blue 6" Stars
Red 3½" x 6½" Points
3½" Corner Squares from Background #2

Six Red 6" Stars
Blue 3½" x 6½" Points
3½" Corner Squares from Background #2

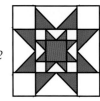

Sewing Top Together

1. Measure several blocks.

2. Cut 3½" Lattice strips into (31) pieces same size as block.

3. Lay out Stars, 3½" Cornerstones, and Lattice.

4. Flip second row right sides together to first, and stack with top pieces on top.

5. Assembly-line sew vertical row together. Repeat with remaining vertical rows. Do not clip connecting threads.

6. Assembly-line sew horizontal rows, pushing seams toward Lattice.

7. Press seams toward Lattice.

Cornerstones can be same fabric as Lattice, or different fabric.

Piecing Strip Border

1. Square off selvages on 2" light and dark strips, and piece together.

2. Make two sets with one and a half strips each for width of quilt.

3. Make two sets with two strips each for length of quilt.

4. Press seams toward darkest strips.

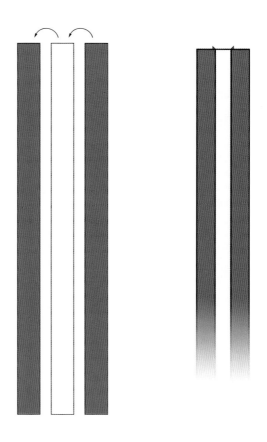

5. Measure quilt, and cut two same width. Cut two same length.

6. Cut (4) 2" segments from left-overs for Nine-Patches.

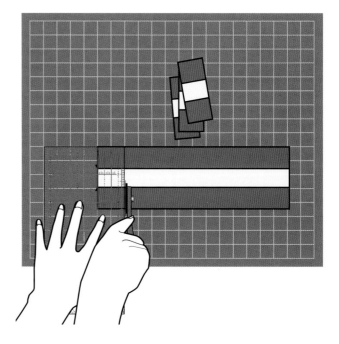

Finishing Nine-Patches

1. Cut (2) 20" pieces from light 2" strip.
   Cut (1) 20" piece from dark 2" strip.

2. Piece 20" strips together lengthwise.
   Press seams toward dark strip.

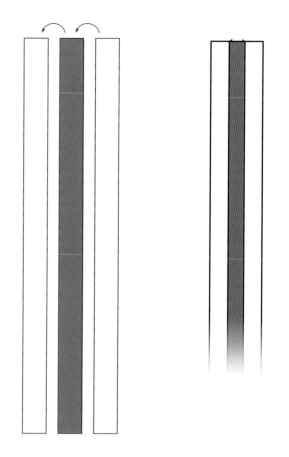

3. Cut (8) 2" segments.

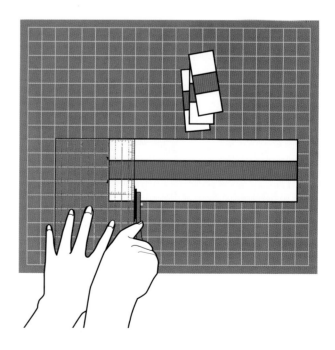

4. Lay out 2" segment in stacks of four, and sew together. Press last seams toward center.

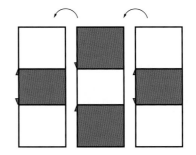

Finishing Top

1. Pin and sew Strip Border to long sides of quilt. Press seams away from quilt.

2. Pin Nine-Patches to ends of remaining Strip Border, and sew. Press seams away from Nine Patches.

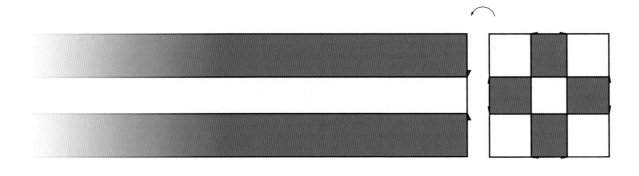

3. Pin and sew Strip Border and Nine-Patches to top and bottom of quilt. Press seams away from quilt.

4. Square off selvages on 6" Outside Border strips, and piece together. Make two sets with one and a half strips each for width of quilt. Make two sets with two strips each for length of quilt.

5. Measure, pin, and sew Outside Border to quilt.

6. Follow **Finishing Instructions** on pages 73 – 77.

Freedom Trail Quilt

Eleanor Burns   *Approximate Finished Size 45" x 45"*

Red   ⅓ yd each or 8 Fat Quarters

Star Centers
(8) different 3½" squares

Star Points
(8) different 6" squares

Solid Squares
(4) different 6½" squares

Side Triangles
(2) different 10" squares

Off-White   ⅞ yd

Star Corners
(4) 2" strips cut into
(64) 2" squares

Star Points
(2) 4½" strips cut into
(16) 4½" squares

Inside Borders
(4) 2" strips

Blue   ⅓ yd each or 8 Fat Quarters

Star Centers
(8) different 3½" squares

Star Points
(8) different 6" squares

Solid Squares
(5) different 6½" squares

Side Triangles
(1) 10" square

Corners
(2) 5½" squares

Blue Print   1¼ yds

Outside Border
(5) 4½" strips

Binding
(5) 3" strips

Finishing

Backing
3 yds

Batting
50" x 50"

The American journey west has shaped our history with a search for freedom and opportunity. Between 1840 and 1870, more than 500,000 emigrants went west along the Great Platte River Road from departure points along the Missouri River. The route used for thousands of years by Native Americans became a thoroughfare for waves of trappers, missionaries, soldiers, farmers, and all sorts of emigrants bound for new territories. Many fell by the way, but many more persevered and went on to build new homes and cities in the West. The quilts they brought must have been welcome reminders of home comforts left behind.

Making Sixteen Stars

1. Place (16) 4½" off white squares right sides together and centered on (8) 6" red squares and (8) 6" blue squares.

Make eight Red Centers   *Make eight Blue Centers*

2. Follow instructions for making dark 2" x 3½" Star Points on pages 6 – 9.

3. At this step, place pairs of same red and same blue patches right sides together, and continue as instructed.

4. Sew eight 6½" Stars together with red centers, and eight with blue centers.

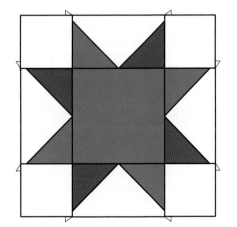 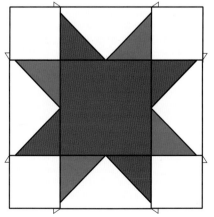

Make eight Blue Centers   *Make eight Red Centers*

Setting Top Together

1. **Side Triangles:** Cut (3) 10" squares on both diagonals. Place in consistent order.

2. **Corner Triangles:** Cut (2) 5½" squares on one diagonal. Place in corners.

Side Triangles   *Corner Triangles*

3. Lay out Stars on point in rows, four across and four down. Alternate between red and blue centers.

4. Place 6½" Solid Squares, alternating reds and blues.

5. Sew together in diagonal rows, matching square corners. Let tips extend.

6. Straighten outside edges, and add 2" Inside Borders.

7. Add 4½" Outside Borders.

8. Follow **Finishing Instructions** on pages 73 – 77.

Old Glory

Approximate Finished Size 22" x 13"   *Teresa Varnes*

According to legend, Betsy Ross is credited with making the first American Flag. George Washington appeared at the doorstep of Mrs. Ross around June 1, 1776, with two members of Congress. They asked her to make a flag from a rough drawing. At Mrs. Ross's suggestion, Washington drew the flag to have a 5-pointed star instead of the 6-pointed star on the original drawing.

Whatever the design, we're proud of Old Glory and its colors – white for purity and innocence, red for valor and hardiness, and blue for perseverance and justice!

Red	¾ yd

(111) 2½" circles

White	¾ yd

(99) 2½" circles

Blue	⅓ yd

(2) 11" x 8½" rectangles

White Star Buttons

(13) ⅝" wide

Making Yo-Yos

1. Make a 2½" circle cardboard template.

2. Trace 2½" circles on fabric and cut out.

3. Thread a hand sewing needle with a double strand of waxed matching thread, and knot.

4. From the wrong side, turn under the raw edge ¼" and run a long gathering stitch near the folded edge.

5. Turn right side out, gather tightly, flatten, and adjust gathers.

6. Knot on front side, or push needle through center, and knot on back.

7. With matching thread and open toe foot, machine sew yo-yos together in rows with wide zig-zag and small stitch length. Optional: Stitch by hand.

Red   (4) rows of 12
                (3) rows of 21

White   (3) rows of 12
                (3) rows of 21

8. Butt rows, and sew together in striped Flag layout.

9. Place blue rectangles right sides together. Sew around outside edge with ¼" seam, leaving opening in middle of 8½" side. Turn right side out. Pin opening shut.

10. Draw 4½" circle on blue rectangle.

11. Place blue rectangle in upper left corner of Flag, with opening on right. Overlap yo-yos, and zig-zag stitch in place.

12. Evenly space and sew thirteen white star buttons.

8½"

11"

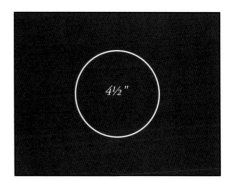

4½"

Finishing

Layering the Quilt

1. Spread out Backing on a table or floor area, right side down. Clamp fabric to edge of table with quilt clips, or tape Backing to floor. Do not stretch Backing.

2. Layer Batting on Backing and pat flat.

3. With quilt right side up, center on Backing. Smooth until all layers are flat. Clamp or tape outside edges.

Safety Pinning

1. Place pin covers on 1" safety pins. Safety pin through all layers three to five inches apart. Pin away from where you plan to quilt.

2. Catch tip of pin in grooves on pinning tool, and close pins.

3. Use pinning tool to open pins when removing them. Store pins opened.

Marking for Free Motion Quilting

Solid squares on Thirteen Colony Quilt and Freedom Trail Quilt are perfect for free motion quilting.

1. Select an appropriate stencil.

2. Center on solid square, and trace lines with disappearing marker. An alternative method is lightly spraying solid square with water, and dusting talc powder into lines.

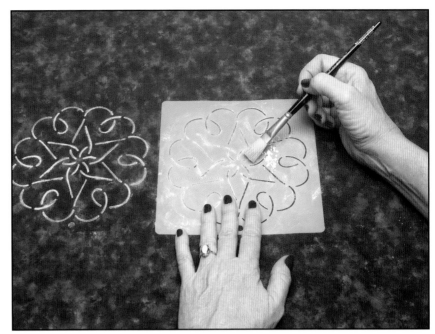

This 6" stencil is #Hol-005-06 from the Stencil Company.

3. Attach darning foot to sewing machine. Drop feed dogs or cover feed dogs with a plate. No stitch length is required as you control the length. Use a fine needle and invisible or regular thread in the top and regular thread to match the Backing in the bobbin. Loosen top tension if using invisible thread.

4. Place hands flat on sides of marking. Bring bobbin thread up on line. Lock stitch and clip thread tails. Free motion stitch around design. Lock stitches and cut threads.

"Stitch in the Ditch" along Lattice, Stars and Borders

1. Thread machine with matching thread or invisible thread. If using invisible thread, loosen top tension. Match bobbin thread to Backing.

2. Attach walking foot, and lengthen stitch to 8 to 10 stitches per inch or 3.5 on computerized machine.

3. Tightly roll quilt to center. Place hands on quilt in triangular shape, and spread seams open. Stitch in the ditch continuously on seam lines. Use needle down feature on sewing machine if available, and pivot with needle in fabric.

4. Stitch around Stars.

Binding

1. Place walking foot attachment on sewing machine and regular thread on top and in bobbin to match Binding.

2. Square off selvage edges, and sew 3" Binding strips together lengthwise. Fold and press in half with wrong sides together.

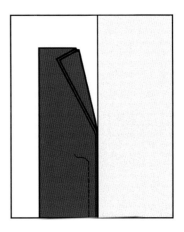

3. Line up raw edges of folded Binding with raw edges of quilt in middle of one side. Begin stitching 4" from end of Binding. Sew with 10 stitches per inch, or 3.0 to 3.5. Sew ⅜" from edge, or width of walking foot.

4. At corner, stop stitching ⅜" in from edge with needle in fabric. Raise presser foot and turn quilt to next side. Put foot back down. Stitch diagonally off edge of Binding.

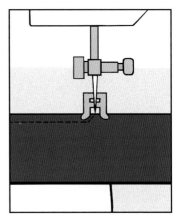

5. Raise foot, and pull quilt forward slightly. Fold Binding strip straight up on diagonal. Fingerpress diagonal fold.

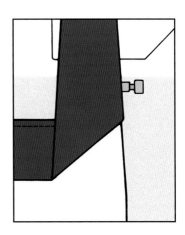

6. Fold Binding strip straight down with diagonal fold underneath. Line up top of fold with raw edge of Binding underneath.

7. Begin sewing from edge.

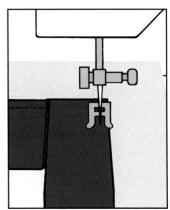

8. Continue stitching and mitering corners around outside of quilt.

9. Stop stitching 4" from where ends will overlap.

10. Line up two ends of Binding. Trim excess with ½" overlap.

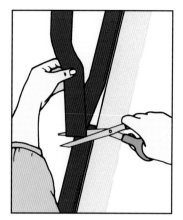

11. Open out folded ends and pin right sides together. Sew a ¼" seam.

12. Continue stitching Binding in place.

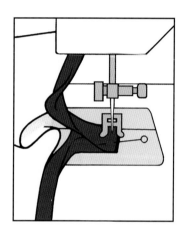

13. Trim Batting and Backing up to ⅛" from raw edges of Binding.

14. Fold Binding to back side of quilt. Pin in place so that folded edge on Binding covers stitching line. Tuck in excess fabric at each miter on diagonal.

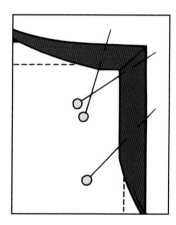

15. From right side, "stitch in the ditch" using invisible thread on front side, and bobbin thread to match Binding on back side. Catch folded edge of Binding on the back side with stitching. Optional: Hand stitch Binding in place.

16. Sew identification label on Back.

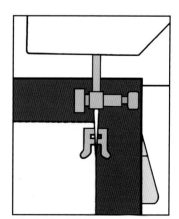

Acknowledgements

Four Star Salute to…

Carol Selepec, Sandy Thompson, and Teresa Varnes.

Index

Order Information

Order these other books from Quilt in a Day that use the Flying Geese Ruler and 6½" Triangle Square Up Ruler. Instructions are included in the packages.

1½" x 3" and 3" x 6" Geese Ruler

6½" Triangle Square Up Ruler

A Star for all Seasons
   6½" Triangle Square Up

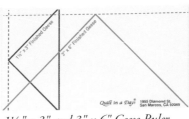
Pioneer Sampler
   3" x 6" Flying Geese Ruler
   4" x 8" Flying Geese Ruler
   6½" Triangle Square Up

Bears in the Woods
   3" x 6" Flying Geese Ruler
   6½" Triangle Square Up

Quilter's Almanac
   6½" Triangle Square Up

Christmas Quilts & Crafts
   3" x 6" Flying Geese Ruler
   4" x 8" Flying Geese Ruler
   6½" Triangle Square Up

Stars Across America
   3" x 6" Flying Geese Ruler
   4" x 8" Flying Geese Ruler
   6½" Triangle Square Up

Country Flag
   6½" Triangle Square Up

Town Square Sampler
   4" x 8" Flying Geese Ruler
   6½" Triangle Square Up

Jewel Box
   6½" Triangle Square Up

Trio of Treasured Quilts
   6½" Triangle Square Up

Quilt in a Day books offer a wide range of techniques and are directed toward a variety of skill levels. If you do not have a quilt shop in your area, you may write or call for a complete catalog and current price list of all books and patterns published by Quilt in a Day®, Inc.

Quilt in a Day®, Inc. • 1955 Diamond Street • San Marcos, CA 92069
1 800 777-4852 • Fax: (760) 591-4424 • www.quiltinaday.com

A Stars & Bars quilt bursts with patriotic colors. Teresa Varnes placed the scrappy stars so that red and blue centers alternate, surrounded by Flying Geese patches and "bars" of a rickrack print. Machine quilting by Carol Selepec adds stipples and stars to the background. The size of this quilt can be adjusted by choosing small or large Flying Geese patches.